Briefly in Spring

Also by Judith E.P. Johnson

Mountain Moods (VDL Publications, 1997)
Gatherers (VDL Publications, 1998)
Fragments (VDL Publications, 2000)
Selected Poems CD (7 RPH, 2001)
Snapshot (Regal Press, 2003)
Landmarks (Ginninderra Press, 2005)
Alone at the Window (Ginninderra Press, 2012)
Between Two Moons (Ginninderra Press, 2015)
Waking from Dreams (Ginninderra Press, 2016)
Where It Leads (Ginninderra Press, 2018)
Only the Waves (Ginninderra Press, 2019)

Judith E.P. Johnson

Briefly in Spring
haiku & senryu

Acknowledgements

The author has had many haiku presented in journals, on radio, and online. The haiku in *Briefly in Spring* are new and unpublished, except for those which appeared in *Echidna Tracks*, *Windfall* and *Ko*.

Special thanks are due to Peter Macrow for his kindness and inspiration, to my children Karen, Debra, and Craig, for their encouragement and support, to Jane Williams for editing this book, and to Katherine Johnson for the cover design.

Briefly in Spring: haiku & senryu
ISBN 978 1 76041 919 6
Copyright © text Judith E.P. Johnson 2020
Cover: Katherine Johnson

First published 2020 by
Ginninderra Press
PO Box 3461 Port Adelaide SA 5015
www.ginninderrapress.com.au

for Graeme

swooping swallow
oh! the swooping swallow
out of sight

from your hand to mine
after your visit
flowers on the table

spring warm
on the air
thoughts of you

three weeks
since you left
your flowers still fresh

small child's piggybank
coins and buttons
spring showers

sparrow's nest
child and I
share the secret

Christmas heatwave
in the post
another snow scene

sun-round
great-grandmother's shortbread
from Scottish snow

balcony breakfast
the sun comes over
my neighbour's roof

sunlit wattles
tiny bee
where is your queen?

buttercups
still they shine
in childhood grasses

derelict house
a tree blossoms
in the chimney

apple orchards
the Sleeping Beauty Range
against stars

overgrown quarry
puddles black
with tadpoles

from the cave's depth
daylight stars
beyond the entrance

New Year's Day
in the recycle bin
last year's calendar

opening the door
I let the old year out
the new year in

old soldier's cottage
geraniums grow
in a wooden leg

dancing
round and round
small child and a butterfly

overnight
wisteria vine
at my window

raspberries
abundant in green leaves
soldier beetles

my feet
in the sand
pulse of the sea

shipwreck bay
a man scans the beach
with a metal detector

sand-coloured
tiny seahorse skeleton
at my feet

star-gazing flounder
only its eyes
in spear light

after the airport
arched bridge
towards the arched mountain

so soft
this long day
not long enough

mountain echo
from the harbour
the ship's long farewell

telling a joke
he laughs
before the punchline

model trains
and film animation
the books of dreams

studying
a sprig of rosemary
on her desk

sun-scorched paddock
once the hush
of gumtrees

wildlife park
devils awake at midday
for the tourists

childhood tree
hidden amongst red berries
a sparrow and I

three small boys cycling
to school
dad runs beside them

back and forth
making up my mind
park swing

gathering wild daffodils
the sunshine
in her arms

blossom shower
tiny green fruit
exposed

garden greengages
the taste of sunshine
and rain

leaving the house
a breeze meets me
with roses

apple blossom
the sun shines
through each petal

granddaughter
on the grey mare
ponytail swinging

sunset glow
grandma
in the red MG

once a plant in a pot
this hedge
I sit under

settling for the night
I leave the tent flap open
for the sunrise

street market
a stallholder
arranges colours of harvest

jack o'lantern
at Halloween
pumpkin soup, pumpkin pie

leafy sunshine
a splash of colour
in the birdbath

birthday barbecue
a sudden breeze
blows out the candles

I tell grandchild
old stories
anew

high squalls
moving in gum trees
the moon and possum eyes

lighting a candle
shadows fill
the darkness

tree-lined street
I walk in and out
of shadows

standing where the bones lie
leaves rattle
around my feet

fog gone
bits of fog
in the hedge

day's work done
I have tea
with the mountain

eventide
the murmur of doves
fills my thoughts

window cleaning
I leave a web
for the spider

on my hand
ladybird, ladybird
gone

how did it get there?
from tree to fence
the spider's thread

country manor house
in and out
the tourists

many have slept there
since great grandmother
cane basinet

homemade doll's house
matchbox furniture
in every room

alone
why is he laughing
the kookaburra

passing through the elms
the wind
takes a leaf

sudden downpour
where from
all these tears

fenced graveyard
grey rabbits
appear and disappear

remote beach
stooping to pick up
a gull's feather

moonlight
crossing a bush track
albino possum pauses

raking
bark and leaves
sound of the sea

in the house
so many empty spaces
since you left

book reading
beside my chair
the dog listens

that warm feeling
this cold day
thoughts of you

calling the cat
the dog
comes too

sunset lighthouse
the long shadow
of white crosses

standing together
the husky's paw
on my foot

only in my dreams
Iceland poppies
out of the flames

from Siberia
the husky runs free
satsuma plum blossom

baby viewing
once
I was there

child's message in a bottle
it returns
with the tide

kiss biscuits
and hold-me-tight sandwiches
lunch with you

on her husband's grave
who from
the red rose?

touching
a beehive
the sun's first light

blocking a hole
in the paling fence
garden gnome still smiling

caught
in the Virginia creeper
sunset

alone
now I can listen
to my thoughts

words on the page
who will hear
my thoughts

new neighbours
how long we have been here
mountain snow

above my quarter acre
all the stars
in place

every day
in the street we pass
no longer

this old song
dancing with you
yesterday

old kettle dies
my friend sends
a sympathy card

cold street
turning a corner
I meet the sun

smell of fresh bread
passing the bakery
I turn back

faded on the page
words of love
from his father

distant voices
I read and reread
old letters

crescent moon
a gravel road
follows the curve of the bay

further and further
away
since you came to my house

afternoon silence
river reeds tremble
with frogs

warm embrace
after you have gone
still there

alone in the dark
I forget
the darkness

young bride and groom
great-grandparents'
wedding photo

fridge magnets
all the places
I have never been

calm river
my father's skipping stone
further than mine

upset
my cup of tea
all over the table

pale moon
two white moths circle
a lantern flame

over tea
we share the contents
of our bundles

flying overhead
a gull's shadow
touches mine

Sphinx Rock
my house and contents
so far below

waiting
for my hair to curl
salon gossip

folded
in a small black evening bag
small black gloves

returning
to old haunts
forgotten feelings

shack nature drawer
all the things
the tide left behind

country road
hand-painted sign
wombat crossing

mortar
holding Georgian bricks together
crushed midden shells

so short
all these long years together
full moon

climate change
she nurses
a new grandchild

new taxi driver
the GPS
in Hindi

distant traveller
home again
before the postcard

church bell
small town Sabbath
everywhere the church bell

under city concrete
old pathways
silent

forgetting
I reach for you
night dreams

home at last
waiting for me
the mountain

stories
at our hearth
poker, tongs and toasting fork

mountains all around
in the surface of the lake
snow clouds

snowy dawn
my potted bulbs
still asleep

seniors' radio
I listen to one love song
after another

grey rain
a snail
inside a June rose

mountain snowman
in the night
who has eaten your nose?

rivulet
tumbling over itself
melted snow

wait! they were here first
pied oystercatcher
and chicks

alone in its shell
a snail comes out
spring mist

rush of winds
where to, where from
the butterfly

breath of flowers
in the darkness
all around me

alive
with sun, moon, stars
and you

briefly
in spring we meet
forget me not

www.ingramcontent.com/pod-product-compliance
Lightning Source LLC
Chambersburg PA
CBHW062201100526
44589CB00014B/1893